The Characters

Margaret Maloney
A mystery writer with a case of writer's block.

J.T. Maloney
Margaret's mystery-seeking daughter.

Dr. Brockett
A would-be scientist short on money.

Carlotta Vanderpepper
A struggling actress on her way to Hollywood.

Jane Crumb
A shy, nervous woman with a neat streak.

Miss Peabody
The devoted owner of the Peabody Hotel.

The Set

Scenes 1-5

The dining/living room of the Peabody Hotel, with Margaret's narrating area downstage right.

Scene 6

Dr. Brockett's bedroom, with Margaret's narrating area downstage right.

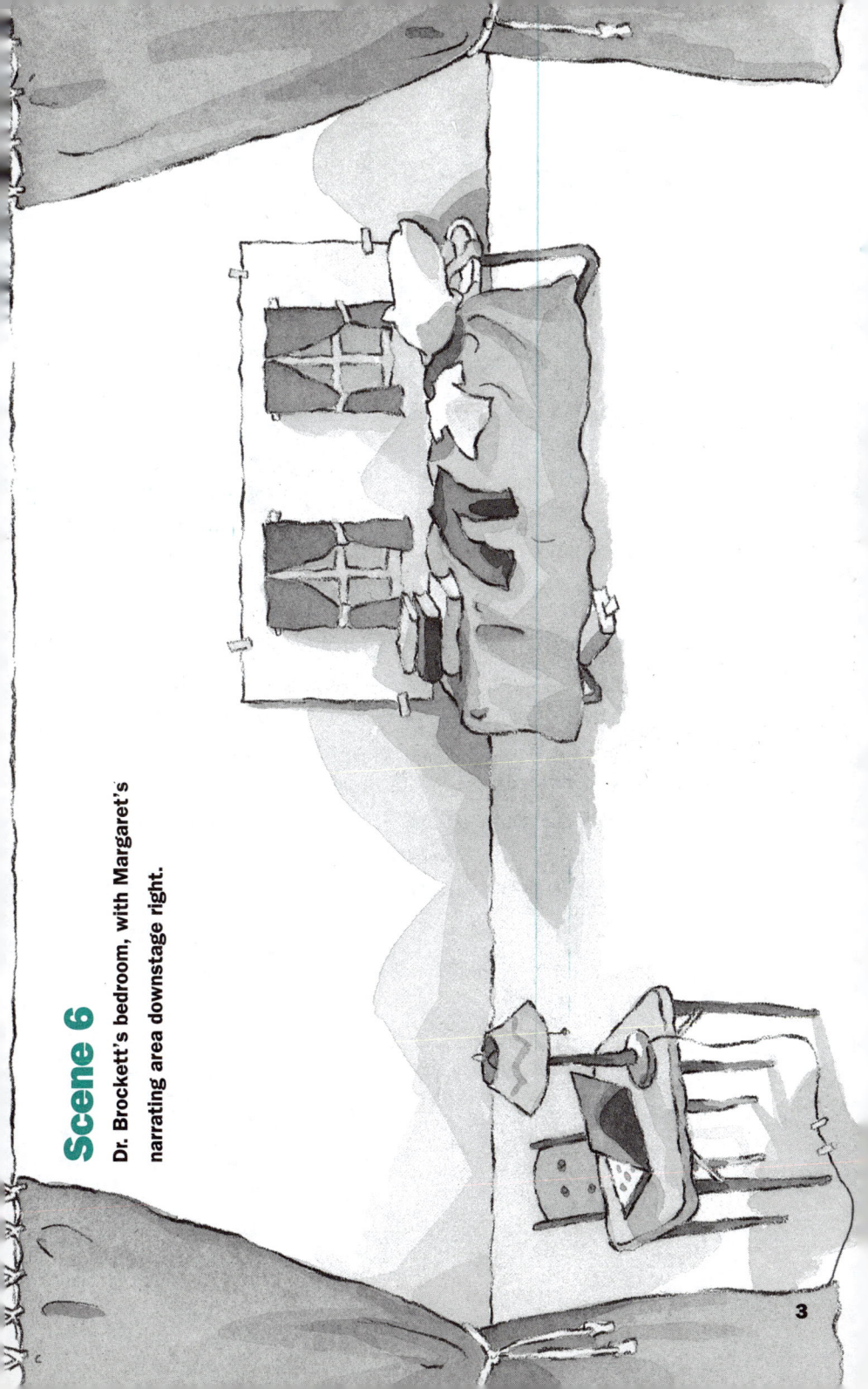

Check Under the Bed

Time *The present.*

At Opening *Miss Peabody and hotel guests are frozen in place stage left in living room of Peabody Hotel. Miss Peabody is standing behind sofa, wringing hands. Jane Crumb is seated quietly on sofa. Dr. Brockett is in chair, reading. Carlotta is standing downstage center, holding beverage with arms outstretched dramatically. Margaret Maloney is downstage right, typing at keyboard. If the actor playing Margaret doesn't want to narrate from memory, she can insert lines into typewriter or tape them to computer screen.*

Scene One

(Margaret begins narrating as she types, looking up now and then, twirling a lock of hair around her finger.)

Margaret Dear Ms. Reed, my FAVORITE editor . . . I know I'm past my deadline, but I think you'll forgive me when you hear the great idea I have for my next mystery book. It's a terrific tale, and it really happened! Remember my daughter, J.T.? She's always wanted to solve a mystery—and now she has. And I slept through the whole thing!

Here's the story: I was having a hard time writing and thought a change of scenery might help. So J.T. and I headed off to our favorite campground. On the way, a terrible storm whipped up. I pulled over till it let up a bit. But when I tried to start the car again, it was dead!

Just down the road was the Peabody Hotel. It was a spooky old place, with dead trees that looked like giant skeletons. Nervously, we walked to the door. The owner, Miss Peabody, greeted us and showed us to our room. I was so tired I went right to sleep, but not J.T. She headed back down to meet the other guests . . . .

Scene Two

(Margaret becomes still as J.T. enters living/dining room area from stage left and other guests "come to life.")

Carlotta So I said, "Mr. Spielberg, darling, puh-LEASE! I simply cannot act with a bunch of dinosaurs!"

Miss Peabody *(Seeing J.T.)* Why, hello! Is anything wrong?

J.T. Oh no, Miss Peabody, I just wasn't sleepy yet.

Miss Peabody Well, come join us.

Dr. Brockett Yes, have a seat. Don't hover in the doorway.

J.T. *(Crossing to couch, sitting down)* Thank you, Mr. . . .

Dr. Brockett That would be DOCTOR, young lady. Dr. Seymore Brockett, scientist, researcher, inventor—

Carlotta And really lazy guy, dedicated to remaining in his chair as much as possible!

Miss Peabody Oh, Carlotta! Dr. Brockett has invented the most amazing thing. Isn't that right, Dr. Brockett?

Dr. Brockett Oh, I hate to toot my own horn—

Carlotta All right, then, we'll talk about ME!

Dr. Brockett —but if you insist. I've invented a remote-control device that allows one to operate an exercise machine without getting up from the couch!

Carlotta (*Sarcastically, rolling her eyes*) Probably comes with a matching snack table and drink holder.

Dr. Brockett Don't be silly. (*To himself*) But that's not a bad idea . . . . (*Gets out pad, jots down idea.*) Anyway, I'm on my way to The Institute of Big Funding to ask for research money. I'm having trouble finding investors.

Miss Peabody (*To J.T.*) Isn't that interesting? (*Pointing to Carlotta*) And this is Carlotta Vanderpepper, the actress!

Carlotta Maybe you've seen some of my pictures. I played an alien in *Planet 99* and, oh, my favorite—I was the lady at the checkout counter in *Supermarket Romance*.

J.T. I don't think I've seen those, Ms. Vanderpepper, but—

Miss Peabody Carlotta is on her way to Hollywood!

Carlotta I've got a BIG part in *Attack of the Killer Bee*. I'm playing the . . . (*striking dramatic pose*) Stung Woman.

Miss Peabody (*Moving to Jane*) And this is Jane Crumb.

Jane (*Shyly*) Miss Peabody, you have a little string on your sleeve. (*Removing it*) There, that's better. (*To J.T.*) Hello. It's nice to meet you. Would you mind taking your shoes off? You're tracking a bit of mud.

Miss Peabody Oh, Jane, don't be silly. I'll clean tomorrow! *(To J.T.)* You'll have to pardon Jane. It's really important to her that everything be . . .

Jane Really, REALLY clean.

Carlotta Oh, listen, everyone! Jane has the most romantic story to tell! Come on, Jane, tell them the story you told me earlier about your fiancé.

Jane Well, I'm engaged to a lovely man named George.

Carlotta WAS engaged! They broke up because George lost his job, and they quarreled about money!

Jane But now I've realized that—

Carlotta *(Interrupting)* Love is more important than money!

Jane Yes. So I'm on my way to—

Carlotta *(Setting glass on coffee table)* She's on her way to meet him so they can patch up their differences. Isn't that the most romantic story?

Jane *(Sighing)* I suppose so. I just hope it all works out. *(Lifts up Carlotta's glass and puts coaster under it.)*

Dr. Brockett Enough gushy stuff. How's an intelligent person supposed to get any reading done around here? That's one of the reasons I stay here, you know. It's usually so quiet. Perhaps the—*(Clears throat.)* "lived in" appearance of the place keeps the regular tourists away.

Miss Peabody (*A little hurt*) I love this place! It's been in my family since the 1800s. My Great Aunt Agatha built it during the California Gold Rush, when people needed a place to stay on their way to and from panning for gold.

Carlotta Oh, Miss Peabody, tell J.T. the story of the gold necklace! It's so romantic!

Miss Peabody (*To J.T.*) You see, there was one gold digger who loved Great Aunt Agatha. He gave her a beautiful gold necklace to remember him by. It's been a treasured family heirloom ever since. (*Beginning to sniffle*) Only now . . . .

Carlotta What's wrong, Miss Peabody?

Miss Peabody Well, I'm afraid the hotel has fallen on hard times. I owe the bank quite a bit of money. So this afternoon, I had to—(*sniffling*) sell Great Aunt Agatha's necklace to raise the money. (*Dabs eyes with tissue.*)

Dr. Brockett What else could you do? You must keep this place open!

Miss Peabody I know. I just hope Great Aunt Agatha understands.

J.T. Understands? She's not still . . .

Miss Peabody Oh no, dear, she's long gone. But I still talk to her. And some nights when the moon is full and the wind is blowing, I swear I hear her talking back. Sometimes she even visits me in my dreams! Oh, listen to me. I sound like a daffy old lady. But tonight I am a bit jumpy.

Carlotta Why, Miss Peabody? Do you think Great Aunt Agatha will be with us this evening?
(Carlotta dances behind Miss Peabody, making ghostly "oooo" sounds.)

Miss Peabody Oh, Carlotta, don't tease! No, it's just that the roads were so bad from the storm today that I couldn't get to the bank to deposit the check. So I've stored it in my secret hiding place. I'm sure it will be safe there, but all the same, I'm nervous.

J.T. A hiding place? Like under the bed, or in a cookie jar?

Miss Peabody Now, J.T., I've said too much already. It's a secret, passed down to me from Great Aunt Agatha!

Carlotta All I can say is, I hope she's quiet if she comes a-haunting. I've had enough trouble sleeping lately!

Dr. Brockett *(Pointing to stack of books on floor)* Why don't you take some of my books, Carlotta, and read until you become drowsy? It always works for me.

Carlotta Well, it doesn't take much to make YOU drowsy! But yes, I think I will borrow some books. Thank you.
(Carlotta picks up stack of books.)

Jane Well, if you'll all excuse me, I think I'll say good night!
(Jane exits stage left, as everyone says good night.)

Carlotta I think I'll turn in as well.

Dr. Brockett I'm going to stay up and read a little longer.

Miss Peabody (*Staring dreamily at Dr. Brockett*) I think I'll sit up a bit with Seymore—er, Dr. Brockett.

Carlotta (*Teasing*) What's this? A budding romance?

Miss Peabody Oh, Carlotta!

Carlotta Well, good night, darlings! (*Carlotta exits stage left.*)

J.T. (*Getting up*) Good night, everyone. I'm a little tired, too. (*J.T. exits stage left, as Dr. Brockett and Miss Peabody wave good night.*)

Miss Peabody (*To Dr. Brockett*) So tell me more about this device! It sounds fascinating! (*Dr. Brockett and Miss Peabody freeze, posing as if in mid-conversation.*)

Scene Three

(*Margaret comes to life, typing at stage right. Dr. Brockett and Miss Peabody exit stage left.*)

Margaret J.T. tiptoed back to bed, careful not to wake me. But she couldn't sleep. She tossed and turned and swore she heard a ghostly voice crying . . . (*Voice from offstage cries "Locket . . . locket . . ."*) Later, she woke to a CRASH! (*Sound effect of crash.*) Now, J.T. claims she tried to wake me at this point, but did she really? Or did she see the chance to solve a mystery all by herself? With me out like a light, she was free to sleuth around on her own!

(*Margaret becomes still again as Miss Peabody and Carlotta take their places. Miss Peabody sits at dining room table, and Carlotta stands behind her holding skillet in one hand, just above Miss Peabody's head. J.T enters from stage left.*)

J.T. (*Rushing in*) Carlotta! What are you doing?

Carlotta (*Flustered*) Oh, hello, darling! You startled me.

Miss Peabody We couldn't sleep, J.T. We're having a snack.

Carlotta I just fried some eggs for us. Want one?

J.T. No, thanks. But what was that crash?

Carlotta (*Still flustered*) A crash? Oh, yes—I dropped the lid to the skillet! Made an awful racket!

Miss Peabody That's probably what woke you up, J.T.

Carlotta I'm sorry! I'll try to be more quiet. Well, I'd better get back in that kitchen and clean up. Otherwise Jane will have a fit in the morning! You two go back to bed. (*Carlotta exits stage right. J.T. and Miss Peabody exit left.*)

Scene Four

(*Margaret comes to life again, typing, as Miss Peabody and Jane take their places. Miss Peabody lies on living room floor, with Jane standing over her.*)

Margaret J.T. headed back to bed, but again she had

trouble sleeping. She had dreams of lockets and Great Aunt Agatha and ghostly tree branches and skillets ready to knock the fried eggs right out of unsuspecting victims. And in the morning, J.T. awoke to the sound of— (*Offstage sound effect of scream*) a scream!

(*Margaret becomes still again. J.T., Dr. Brockett, and Carlotta rush in from stage left, wearing bathrobes.*)

J.T. Jane! I heard a—(*Sees Miss Peabody.*) Miss Peabody! Are you all right? (*Rushes over to her.*)

Carlotta Miss Peabody! What are you doing on the floor?

Dr. Brockett My goodness, what is going on here? Are you all right, Elizabeth—I mean, Miss Peabody?

Jane The poor thing! She seems to be out cold!

J.T. Miss Peabody! Can you hear me? (*To Jane*) What happened?

Jane I haven't a clue! I heard a scream, and when I came in— (*Miss Peabody begins to stir.*)

Miss Peabody (*Moaning groggily*) The money . . . gone . . . .

Jane I'll go get a wet cloth for her head. (*Exits stage right.*)

J.T. Miss Peabody, it's J.T.! Are you all right?

Miss Peabody (*Sitting up*) I think so . . . . (*Regaining her senses*) But the check! It's missing!

J.T. How could that be? Tell me where you hid it, and then maybe I can help you look for it!

Miss Peabody NO! I can't possibly tell—it's a secret! (*Jane enters with wet cloth.*)

Jane Here, put this on your head.
(*Jane tries to apply cloth, but Miss Peabody resists.*)

Miss Peabody (*Struggling to get up*) The check is here someplace—I'll just have to find it. But first, help me up. I must get breakfast started.

Carlotta Oh, Miss Peabody, don't be silly! Go lie down for a little while! Jane and I will fix breakfast.

Miss Peabody No. As long as this is my hotel, breakfast is my responsibility. Help me to the kitchen and then go get yourselves dressed. I'll be fine, thank you.

(Carlotta and Jane help Miss Peabody up and then exit stage right. Dr. Brockett turns to leave, but J.T. detains him.)

J.T. (*Twirling lock of hair*) Dr. Brockett, I have a question.

Dr. Brockett Yes, J.T.?

J.T. I know that you and Miss Peabody stayed up last night later than the rest of us.

Dr. Brockett Yes, we did.

J.T. Did she happen to mention the location of her secret hiding place to you?

Dr. Brockett No. What are you driving at, young lady? Surely you don't think that I—

J.T. I'm not accusing you of anything, sir. I just thought that since you two had a private conversation last night, and since she seems to "admire" you so much—

Dr. Brockett Well, you can't blame her for THAT!

J.T. I just thought she might have given you a little hint about where she hid the check.

Dr. Brockett I can see you think you're a real junior sleuth, J.T. Maloney, but you'll have to look a little further. I'm not the culprit—I'm fond of Miss Peabody and would never harm a hair on her head. Now if you'll excuse me, I'd like to get ready for breakfast.
(Exits stage left. J.T. stays onstage, pacing and twirling a lock of hair.)

J.T. *(To herself)* This is great! A real mystery to solve, and my mom didn't even make it up! Now, who could have stolen that check? Could it have been Dr. Brockett? He could be pretending to like Miss Peabody just to steal her money for his research. Maybe she's so love-struck that she told him where it was hidden and doesn't even remember. Hmm . . . . But what about Carlotta? She must really need the money if she's willing to travel across the country to play the role of the "Stung Woman"! And she was alone with Miss Peabody last night—what would she have done with that skillet if I hadn't walked in?! But what about Jane Crumb? She and her fiancé could sure use the money. One thing's for sure, whoever stole the check will be getting out of here fast. I bet more will be revealed at breakfast. I'd better get dressed and get back to the scene of the crime, 'cause I'm—*(striking a pose)* J.T. Maloney, Master Detective!
(Exits stage left.)

Scene Five

(Dishes and cups are placed on dining room table. Carlotta and Dr. Brockett enter from stage left and sit at table. Miss Peabody enters from stage right and walks around pouring coffee. Jane follows her, wiping up spills before taking a seat.)

J.T. *(Entering)* Hello again, everybody!

Miss Peabody Hello, J.T. Where is your mother? Isn't she having breakfast?

J.T. No, she says she's sorry. She finally had an idea for her new mystery novel this morning. She wants to work on it while she's feeling inspired.

Carlotta Maybe your mother will write a screenplay for ME to star in someday! And speaking of me, you'll never guess what's happened!

Dr. Brockett Oh, let me see. They're remaking *Gone With the Wind* and they want you to play the wind.

Carlotta Very funny. No, listen! I just got a call from my agent! They're going to start filming the movie sooner than they thought, and I must dash off tomorrow! I'm sorry to leave you in a pinch, Miss Peabody.

J.T. (*Suspiciously*) That's odd. I didn't hear the phone ring.

Carlotta That's because it was my cell phone. I keep it in my purse at all times, with the ringer on low. You never know when that big break is gonna come! Anyway, Miss Peabody, I'm sure that check will turn up soon and everything will be all right.

Miss Peabody (*Disappointed*) I'm sure it will.

Carlotta So let me tell you more about this movie . . . .

(*Margaret begins narrating and typing as Carlotta pantomimes blabbing to other guests.*)

Margaret Now J.T.'s detective wheels were really turning. She waited until Carlotta was so busy telling everyone about her new movie that no one noticed her slip away. (*J.T. exits stage left unnoticed.*) She crept off to Carlotta's room and began snooping. But all she found were some old movie scripts, false eyelashes, and a box of newspaper clippings. She crept back to the table.

(*The characters begin speaking as Margaret becomes still and J.T. enters from stage left.*)

Carlotta —and that's when I say my line, "You might sting me, bee, but you'll never break my spirit!"

Dr. Brockett (*Using J.T.'s entrance to cut off Carlotta*) Why, J.T., where did you scoot off to? Look everyone, it's J.T.!

J.T. Yes, I was just checking on my mom.

Carlotta Well, you missed my performance of the big "swarm" scene.

Dr. Brockett It was quite a scene, all right. And now, if you'll excuse me, I must go look over my proposal. (*Quickly exits stage left.*)

Carlotta And I must go pack. Can't keep Hollywood waiting, you know! I want to leave first thing tomorrow. (*Exits bouncily, stage left.*)

Miss Peabody (*Getting up to clear dishes*) I do hope she doesn't check out until after we've found the money. I'm so worried! I sold the necklace, and now I have nothing!

J.T. Miss Peabody, was the necklace by any chance a locket?

Miss Peabody No, dear, why do you ask?

J.T. Oh, I just thought I heard somebody talking about a locket last night.

Miss Peabody That's odd. No, it was a beautiful chain with a gold nugget the size of a walnut. A priceless piece! (*Begins to sniffle and exits stage right, carrying dishes.*)

Jane (*Nervously wiping table with rag*) Poor Miss Peabody! That check just has to turn up!

J.T. (*Twisting lock of hair*) Jane, may I ask you something?

Jane (*Seeming more nervous*) Of course.

J.T. How is it that you were the first one in the living room this morning when Miss Peabody screamed?

Jane I just heard her and came running. Why? What are you accusing me of?

J.T. Nothing! But tell me . . . do you maybe have some idea of Miss Peabody's secret hiding place? Maybe you've come across it cleaning up?

Jane (*Clearly upset now*) No! Now, if you'll excuse me, I need to go tidy up my room.

J.T. (*To herself*) Hmm! Jane clearly has something to hide.

Scene Six

(*Margaret comes to life again, typing, as scenery is changed to Dr. Brockett's room.*)

Margaret The rest of the day was uneventful. I worked on my new book, which was going nowhere—just like our car. J.T. was thrilled. The longer we were stuck there, the longer she had to solve the mystery. But that night, things really got spooky. We were both sound asleep when once

again J.T. heard a ghostly voice, this time saying . . .
(*Voice from offstage cries "Locket . . . Brockett . . . locket!"*)
She crept out of bed and into the hallway just in time to see Dr. Brockett headed downstairs with his book and pipe. She knew where SHE was headed next—Dr. Brockett's bedroom!
(*J.T. enters from stage left, wearing bathrobe.*)

J.T. (*Looking around*) Now, let's see. Is there anything here that shouldn't be here? . . . What's this? (*Picks up book from under his bed.*) "The Case of the Lost Locket"—LOCKET? Like the voice keeps saying!

Dr. Brockett (*From offstage*) Fiddlesticks—I must have left my glasses in my room.

J.T. Uh oh, I'd better hide!
(*J.T. dives under bed, clutching book. Dr. Brockett enters from stage left, walks around lifting pillows and clothes, searching for glasses. Finally finds glasses in his pocket.*)

Dr. Brockett (*To himself*) In your own pocket, Brockett! Honestly, you'd lose your head if it wasn't so . . . brilliant!
(*Dr. Brockett exits stage left, chuckling to himself.*)

J.T. (*Coming out from under bed*) That was way too close. (*Looks at book.*) "The Case of the Lost Locket." Could it be just a coincidence? (*Thumbs through pages, finds the check.*) The check! (*Shouting*) Miss Peabody! Come quick! I've found your check!

Dr. Brockett (*Entering from stage left*) What is the meaning of this, young lady? What are you doing in my room?

J.T. I'd like to ask you, Dr. Brockett, what is the meaning of THIS? (*Waves the check at him.*)

Dr. Brockett I have no idea. Is that Miss Peabody's check?!

J.T. Yes, and I'm wondering why it was under YOUR bed!

Dr. Brockett I assure you, I have no idea!
(*Carlotta and Jane enter from stage left, running.*)

Carlotta Dr. Brockett, what's going on?? Hey! That's one of the books you lent me! "The Case of the Lost Locket."

Jane And what's that, J.T.? The lost check?

J.T. Yes. It was in this book!

Carlotta Looks pretty bad, Dr. B. What do you have to say for yourself?
(*All eyes turn to Dr. Brockett.*)

Dr. Brockett I say, rubbish! That is not my book!

Carlotta Oh yes it is! That's one of the books you lent me last night to help me fall asleep.

Dr. Brockett Look inside it. Does it have one of my personalized bookplates?!

J.T. (*Looks inside book.*) No. It says "Agatha Peabody."

Carlotta Now I'm completely confused. I know you gave me that book last night, Dr. Brockett. And I returned it to your room this morning, right after my agent called. (*Everyone looks at Dr. Brockett again.*)

Dr. Brockett Ladies, ladies, don't be silly! Suppose for a moment I did steal the check—why would I stash it in a book and then lend that book to Carlotta?

Jane I'm afraid I can answer a few questions. Miss Peabody has been so nice to me, but, well, she just never cleans up properly! So the other night I thought I'd straighten up a little. I was on my hands and knees looking for lint when I noticed that book under the sofa. I assumed it was one of Dr. Brockett's, so I placed it on his stack of books, and that's when J.T. and her mom arrived.

Carlotta And then Dr. Brockett gave the books to me.

Jane Yes—and I sneaked back down early the next morning to finish cleaning, which is why I was the first person in the living room when Miss Peabody screamed. (*Miss Peabody enters from stage left.*)

Miss Peabody What's going on? (*Spies book.*) My Great Aunt Agatha's book! And my check!! You found them! I always stash important papers on page 99 of that book and hide it under the sofa. But how did it get here?

Jane It's a long story.
(*All nod in agreement, chuckling.*)

Dr. Brockett I have one question, Miss Maloney. What made you look in MY room?

J.T. Let's just say . . . a little voice told me to do it.
(*Everyone looks puzzled, shrugging. All then exit together stage left. Margaret comes to life again, typing.*)

Margaret In the morning J.T. filled me in on what had happened. Of course, she's convinced it was Great Aunt Agatha who led her to the book, but I explained it was surely just Miss Peabody talking in her sleep. But there was one more odd thing. The next night, I dreamed Great Aunt Agatha told me to give my car another try. So, goofy as I felt, I went down the next day to start the engine. And guess what—it worked! I'm sure the cables had just finally dried out. But that's not what J.T. thought! Anyway, dear Editor, I'd better finish this letter so I can start writing my next bestseller: *Check Under the Bed,* starring . . . (*J.T. enters from stage left, striking pose*) J.T. Maloney, Master Detective!

The End